1st Recital Series

FOR MALLET PERCUSSION

Including works of:
- James Curnow
- Craig Alan
- Mike Hannickel
- Ann Lindsay

Solos for Beginning
through Early Intermediate
level musicians

CURNOW®
MUSIC

EXCLUSIVELY DISTRIBUTED BY

HAL•LEONARD®
CORPORATION

7777 W. BLUEMOUND RD. P.O. BOX 13819 MILWAUKEE, WI 53213

Edition Number: CMP 0853.03

1st Recital Series
Solos for Beginning through Early Intermediate level musicians
Mallet Percussion

ISBN: 90-431-1915-6

CD Accompaniment tracks performed by Becky Shaw

CD number: 19.040-3 CMP

Foreword

High quality solo/recital literature that is appropriate for performers playing at the Beginner through Early Intermediate skill levels is finally here! Each of the **1st RECITAL SERIES** books is loaded with exciting and varied solo pieces that have been masterfully composed or arranged for your instrument.

Included with the solo book is a professionally recorded CD that demonstrates each piece. Use these examples to help develop proper performance practices. There is also a recording of the accompaniment alone that can be used for performance (and rehearsal) when a live accompanist is not available. A separate Piano Accompaniment book is available [edition nr. CMP 0857.03].

Though the solos in this book can be played on any available Mallet Percussion instrument, we suggest using the following instruments when possible:

Bells: #1, 2, 3, 5, 7, 11

Xylophone: #4, 6, 8, 9, 10, 12

Table of Contents

Track | | Page

1 2   Kaitlin's Music Box 5

3 4   The Koi Pond 6

5 6   Just As I Am 7

7 8   The Can-Can 8

9 10   Grandfather's Clock 9

11 12   The Entertainer 10

13 14   Arioso 11

15 16   Along Came A Spider 12

17 18   Pizzicati From "Sylvia" 13

19 20   Funeral March Of A Marionette 14

21 22   String Quartet # 2 15

23 24   Rondeau 16

⬜   *Solo with accompaniment*

⬛   *Accompaniment*

MALLET PERCUSSION **1. KAITLIN'S MUSIC BOX** **Ann Lindsay** (ASCAP)

2. THE KOI POND

Craig Alan (ASCAP)

Track
5 6 MALLET PERCUSSION

W.D.Bradbury and C. Elliott
3. JUST AS I AM

Arr. **Mike Hannickel** (ASCAP)

Jacques Offenbach
4. THE CAN-CAN
Arr. **Craig Alan** (ASCAP)

Henry Clay Work

5. GRANDFATHER'S CLOCK

MALLET PERCUSSION

Mike Hannickel (ASCAP)

Scott Joplin
6. THE ENTERTAINER

MALLET PERCUSSION

Arr. **Ann Lindsay** (ASCAP)

Copyright © 2003 by **Curnow Music Press, Inc.**

J.S.Bach
7. ARIOSO

Arr. **Craig Alan** (ASCAP)

8. ALONG CAME A SPIDER

MALLET PERCUSSION

Mike Hannickel (ASCAP)

Note: All glissandos are naturals ("white-keys")

Copyright © 2003 by **Curnow Music Press, Inc.**

Leo Delibes
9. PIZZICATI from "SYLVIA"

MALLET PERCUSSION

Arr. **Ann Lindsay** (ASCAP)

Charles Gounod

10. FUNERAL MARCH OF A MARIONETTE

Arr. **Ann Lindsay** (ASCAP)

MALLET PERCUSSION

* All rolls are optional

Alexander Borodin
Theme from

MALLET PERCUSSION **11. STRING QUARTET #2**

"Nocturne"

Arr. **James Curnow** (ASCAP)

Jean Joseph Nouret
12. RONDEAU
Arr. **James Curnow** (ASCAP)